DAVID PLOWDEN

INDUSTRIAL LANDSCAPE

THE CHICAGO HISTORICAL SOCIETY

in Association with

W · W · NORTON & COMPANY   NEW YORK / LONDON

OTHER BOOKS BY DAVID PLOWDEN

An American Chronology

Steel

Wayne County: The Aesthetic Heritage of a Rural Area
(with Stephen Jacobs)

The Iron Road
(with Richard Snow)

Desert and Plain, the Mountains and the River
(with Berton Roueché)

Tugboat

Commonplace

Bridges: The Spans of North America

Cape May to Montauk
(with Nelson P. Falorp)

Floor of the Sky

The Hand of Man on America

Nantucket
(with Patricia Coffin)

Lincoln and His America

Farewell to Steam

DAVID PLOWDEN

INDUSTRIAL LANDSCAPE

THE CHICAGO HISTORICAL SOCIETY

in Association with

W · W · NORTON & COMPANY   NEW YORK / LONDON

For Sandra

The text of this book is composed in Bodoni.
Composition by Zimmering & Zinn, Inc.
Manufacturing by Balding + Mansell.
Book design by Christine Aulicino.

First Edition

Library of Congress Cataloging in Publication Data

Plowden, David.
Industrial landscape.

1. Photography, Industrial—Illinois—Chicago.
2. Chicago (Ill.)—Description—Views.   I. Title.
TR706.P56   1985   779'.4'0924   85-309

ISBN 0-393-01992-6

W. W. Norton & Company, Inc., 500 Fifth Avenue, New York, N.Y. 10110
W. W. Norton & Company Ltd., 37 Great Russell Street, London WC1B 3NU

1 2 3 4 5 6 7 8 9 0

"Make no little plans. They have no magic to stir men's blood," said Daniel Burnham when urging Chicagoans to adopt his master plan for the city. However, Burnham might as well have been speaking for all America, not just of Chicago. His exhortation addresses one of the most American of American characteristics. Given the chance we have rarely, if ever, made "little plans."

And why should it be any other way? We are a huge country, most of which until very recently was virgin territory by the standards of the rest of the Western world. Until very recently, too, we were preoccupied with ourselves almost exclusively, turning our attention to the business of settling and conquering our own country, which, although much less so than a century ago, is still richly endowed with natural resources and land. Even today, after nearly four hundred years of continual, uninterrupted settlement, in spite of all we have taken from it and all the transformations we have wrought upon its surface, there is still more public domain than private in which to explore. In the far reaches of the western ranges, particularly, one often has the feeling that we have just arrived there and have had hardly a chance to unpack, so close is the sense of the frontier.

It has been said in a hundred ways before that the course of American history has to a great extent been directed by the magnitude of its geography and its material and human resources. And it is true, I believe, that more than anything else, ours is a history of enterprise; of the ways in which we have sought to utilize our extraordinary endowments. All our greatest achievements, when measured against those of other peoples, have most often been in the realm of science and technology; the practical and profitable application of solutions to problems. We are by now old hands at overcoming the obstacles of space and time—whether inner or outer. We are a nation that prides itself on covering the distance and getting things done—quickly.

It is no wonder, then, that America has earned the reputation of being The Motherland of Industry, as she has been called. Sometimes we seem to be more an engine than a nation, always in motion, driven by some inner source of kinetic energy; or like an intricately coordinated organism running on and on, consuming ourselves to feed the fires that drive us onward, always reaching further and further.

We are, I think, still driven by that same belief in our manifest destiny as we were in the middle of the last century when the phrase was coined. We are still "compelled to overspread the continent...for the free development of our yearly multiplying millions."

•   •   •

"The business of America is business," Calvin Coolidge said with characteristic brevity in 1925. And perhaps there is no better place to look at the "business of America" than in Chicago. More than any other city Chicago has epitomized the essence of the American character, a fact not lost on observers from abroad and many Americans—not to mention Chicagoans of themselves. No matter who pens the words, Chicago is never described in timid terms. "Brash," "burly," "raw," "proud," "young," "coarse," "audacious," "fabulous," and "energetic" typically describe this place.

Kipling, who was not exactly taken with Chicago, said: "Having seen it, I urgently desire never to see it again. It is inhabited by savages." Perhaps he felt the same way about America, because he also described Chicago as being "the most American of American cities." Speaking of his visit here he said, however, that he had "struck a city—a real city." Yet not all British visitors felt as Kipling. One, Sara Jane Lippincott, called it "the lightning city" and went on to say that "the growth of this city is one of the most amazing things in the history of modern times."

Chicago was obviously driven by its own particular manifest destiny, a fact of which Newton Dent, writing in *Munsey's* magazine in 1907, was aware. "Nothing that either man or nature can do, apparently, can check the growth of this city that has spread back from the lake like a prairie fire, until its great bulk covers nearly two hundred square miles of Illinois." Moving into high gear, he said,

> ...she is the first city of the world in many things—in enterprise, in growth, in energy, and in her indomitable optimism and self confidence. Nowhere else is there such human voltage.
>
> "Bring me your lumber," she demands, "I want two billion feet of it a year. Bring me every weekday fifty thousand of your farm animals and a million bushels of your grain. Bring your ore and oil, cloth and paper and tobacco, and be quick, for I am Chicago—the city of speed."

But Carl Sandburg, of course, said it best of all:

> . . . come and show me another city with lifted head singing so proud to be alive and coarse and strong and cun-

ning. . . . Bareheaded, Shoveling, Wrecking, Planning, Building, Raking, Rebuilding, . . . Laughing in the stormy, husky, bawling laughter of youth, half-naked, sweating, proud to be Hog Butcher, Tool Maker, Stacker of Wheat, Player with Railroads and Freight Handler to the nation.

The city and the world of Sandburg exist no longer. He spoke of the "Golden Age" of American industry—if one can use such a term to describe an age of iron and steam. His was a time of enormous self-confidence, when we were able to reap the full benefits—and along with them suffer the horrors—of the Industrial Revolution. It was a time that produced works every bit as robust and magnificent in scope as the aspirations of the people who built them. There was nothing faint-hearted or tentative about the way Americans or Chicagoans then tackled the tasks at hand, or about the people who accomplished them. Our industrial machinery had been honed to perfection. It was in magnificent shape, like the muscles of a long-distance runner.

That was the same age that produced a thousand grand and useful works: the rolling mills in Lackawanna and Gary and Braddock, the monstrous grain elevators in Duluth and Enid and Buffalo, and the ore docks on Lake Superior; the Panama Canal, the Brooklyn Bridge, and the Union Stockyards; the building of the Great Northern Railway, the Northern Pacific, the Santa Fe; and it was the age of the great four-stack ocean liners. It was a time of steam locomotives and boiler plates and blast furnaces; it was a time also of mining and lumber kings and oil and cattle barons; of Sir Henry Bessemer's Converter, of Jim Hill and E. H. Harriman; of Richard Sears and Alvah Roebuck. It was an age of the ruthless, too, of Carnegie and Frick and Rockefeller and Morgan and robber barons; of Insull and Jay Gould and visionaries, too, like Jay's son George; and of those with concern for others, like Debs and the Reuther brothers.

It was a time of great inventions, inventions that transformed our way of life and led to the mechanization of almost every aspect of human endeavor—John Deere's moldboard plow, the McCormick reaper, the power loom, the sewing machine, the Westinghouse air brake, the assembly line, and the automobile.

Perhaps at no other time was the evidence of our industrial strength more forcefully expressed than by the machinery and factories of the period from the late nineteenth century to the Great Depression of the thirties. Nor was the significance of these forms lost on the architects of the day. In 1913 Walter Gropius said that "the grain elevators . . . the

coal conveyors of the great railway lines and the more modern industrial plants of North America are almost as impressive in their monumental power as the buildings of ancient Egypt." Yet as monumental as these structures may be, they have little in common with those of an ancient and unmechanized world. Ours are vital works, not the products of pretend gods, but those of ordinary people and meant for the world of the living, not the hereafter.

It is ironic to think that cities like Pittsburgh, Duluth, Detroit, Buffalo, and Birmingham—and the industrial areas of Chicago, places made by coal and iron and sweat—have come to symbolize so many of our aspirations. These places are not gentle. The new workplace may be bland and sterile but by comparison the old was like a war zone, where laborers were asked to pit themselves against appalling dangers and filth and noise. "It is a terrible and beautiful thing to make iron," wrote Thomas Bell in his epic novel of life in a steel town, *Out of This Furnace.* "It is honest work, too, work the world needs. . . . the men working with that burning iron seemed like heroes. . . ." I know a little, just enough, of what he speaks, if only as an observer, for I have been in enough of those places to see the effects of our industrialization from that point of view. I haven't as yet found out about the horrors of hell firsthand, but my image of it could not be more frightening and fiery than that of places like cast houses and around the furnaces, where on a daily basis men have to confront and deal with the dangers of working with white-hot metal.

Out of all the times I have been in the mills photographing, I remember one incident in particular. I was taking pictures of a group of men "slagging" a row of ingots—throwing the unwanted slag off the top of the molten iron within the molds. The men, all dressed in silver greatcoats and masks and gauntlets that were meant to protect them from the heat, were working on a narrow parapet practically on top of the boiling metal itself. As I watched I was struck by the primitive nature of their work, especially so when gauged by the standards of the times; we are, after all, on the threshold of the twenty-first century. The space they worked in, too, belonged to another time. It was almost medieval, like a cavern, and beyond the metal, which provided the only illumination as far as I could tell, it was black and filled with acrid smoke. Here and there the light from the fires caught the flanks of huge metallic vessels lurking there.

To do their job the men used wooden boards that they would shove into the liquid metal on top of the molds. Then, using them like shovels, they would twist and turn them in order to throw off the unwanted slag. In so doing they created a shower of sparks that rained down on everything, including themselves. The boards, being of wood, of course caught fire each time they were inserted into the metal and had to be discarded after only a few minutes. The men worked at a feverish pace, more so, I was told later, because of my presence, and with seemingly little regard for danger.

After they had finished, one of them, a towering and heavyset man, a Mexican, came over to me with a great smile on his face. "You want to see something?" he asked, ripping open the buttons of his greatcoat and then the top ones of his union suit (although it was July, like all steel workers he wore his long johns year-round as insulation both against the wintry blasts outside and the heat of the white-hot metal inside). Then, pointing to his bare chest with both hands, he said, grinning proudly, "Mosquito bites, mosquito bites." I looked. His skin, in spite of the mandatory protective clothing, was completely covered with little scars and patches of seared flesh made by the hot sparks—battle ribbons from years on the front.

I often think of that man and the others like him in the mills and wonder if his fellow workers in Centex Industrial Park will have the same sense of pride or battle scars to show when it's time to take their pensions. And, too, I often think of him when I remember the role of Pullman in the vicious strike that bears his name and of those of Frick and the Pinkertons at Homestead, and the bleeding faces afterward. I know now the necessity for all the bars that line the streets leading from the Mill Gates.

I also remember a remark that a conservative old farmer made over a cup of coffee in a café in Iowa not so long ago. We were discussing the high price of farm machinery and just about everything else. Like so many others, he fixed upon the cost of labor as the whipping boy for the ills of our economy. At one point he stopped and looked straight at me. "Hell," he said, "you know, you wouldn't get me to work in one of those places no matter how much you paid me."

•   •   •

"I KNOW THAT PLACE." I've heard that comment a hundred times from people who look at my photographs of industrial places, who have never set foot on that particular piece of ground; have never seen them except in my prints.

An assembly line works on the same principle whether producing tractors in Waterloo, Iowa, or Fords in Dearborn, Michigan. And equally important, they all look alike. Pictures of factory workers hunched over drill presses or lathes rarely give a clue to the nature of the work they are performing. The look of industrial places, for the most part, is almost always the same everywhere. Industry, like agriculture, has its own generic landscape.

There are few places I know of that present a more graphic picture of an entirely manmade landscape than on the island of Manhattan and in the industrial environs of Chicago. Both are complete and infinite; totally fabricated environments. Each in its own way is almost on the same scale of magnitude as the Grand Canyon.

One afternoon while looking for places to photograph I found myself on top of a hill made from man's debris somewhere west of Whiting, Indiana. It was one of the few places that rose far enough above the plain to allow me to get a perspective on things. I looked and for as far as I could see in each direction, from horizon to horizon, there was nothing there that had not been made by man; nothing that had not been put to use at one time or another for his purpose.

The air was smoky, a hopeful sign there, for it meant that "times were good," that there were jobs. And as I looked I saw the source: the smokestacks venting sooty clouds at intervals into the sky. I remembered another time on the roof of a factory building looking out over much the same place and seeing a huge black cloud composed of obviously vile and noxious gasses fill the sky over South Chicago. "Now isn't that a beautiful sight?" I heard one of the men who was guiding me say to the other. He knew what "hard times" were; he was a second-generation steel worker.

From my hilltop I listened. There was not a moment without the sounds of machinery, the growl and clanging of industry, somewhere. The hum of engines came from a hundred unseen places. And as I listened more carefully I could tell where the different sounds came from—the steel mills, the flour mills, the furnaces, the refineries, the trucks, and the railroad yards.

I looked north and there in the distance some twenty miles away was the Loop, as always so small and diminished by what lay around it in the foreground. I began to hear the sounds of children's voices coming from a field overrun with rampant waste and debris. Beyond the children rose the towers of the refinery like an unfinished skeletal city; beyond that, a phalanx of towers of a different sort were layered one upon the other. The inscrutable, complicated architecture of steel making.

To my right were acres of tank farms filled with huge bulbous vessels that spread away into the industrial haze. Around the tanks the ground was black as tar. Further on in the distance to the west there were more stacks and strange shapes struck against the sky like giant chessmen arranged on a board. Before them in the middle ground the sun shone off the roofs of what seemed like miles, square miles, of long, metal sheds slinking along the ground filling up what little empty space there might have been. And everywhere there were wires—power lines running to and fro—connecting everything in sight.

By most standards the view shouldn't have been beautiful, and to many it probably wouldn't have been, but to me it was in some darkly compelling way. Perhaps it was because man had made this place so entirely his own that it was poignant and frightening at the same time. Frightening because man seemed so completely in command of the situation and able to change the face of the land at will and in such a short space of time. Poignant because all this is so obviously illusory in the framework of cosmic time.

As I looked toward the western sky I was struck too by the fact that man's works were the only vertical elements to be seen. On that tiny interface between the land and the sky we had wrought a transformation, but one that was only of significance to us. Suddenly all that smoke pouring forth from those stacks, which so gladdened the hearts of the mill owners and factory workers, took on another, more far-reaching meaning, whose implications went beyond the short-term ones that affect the economy. The effects of that smoke would be felt long after what was in the foreground was in ruins. Looking at the juxtaposition of industry and the sky it was impossible not to think about such things as acid rain and the greenhouse effect and all of those other, very real and controversial problems that are the direct result of our industrialization.

That place, like so many similar ones throughout America, represented an archeological site, albeit an incomplete one, whose top layer is still being laid down. It was all there, industry and decay, energy and ambition, success and failure randomly strewn across thousands of acres of land as far as the eye could see. Taken as a whole the cumulative evidence presented by that ground revealed much about our aspirations and our priorities. What was laid out there was not a showcase, a conscious effort at projecting an image, as places like the mall in Washington, Fifth Avenue in New York, or the magnificent mile in Chicago are, but a working landscape; a much truer gauge of our civilization, I believe.

•   •   •

FROM THE MOMENT our forebears stumbled ashore at Jamestown and Plymouth, we have always been on a frontier of one kind or another, be it geographical or technological. We have continually been asked to put our ingenuity to work in coping with the problems of this immense and diverse land. In the process we have altered many times our course and the way we look as a country. Change has become an integral part of our culture. By now it is taken for granted that things will not be the same tomorrow; that the sun will always dawn on a new and different world.

Today we have come upon one of those periodic watersheds in our history, one that, by all indications, may well have more far-reaching effects on our culture and economy than anything since the Industrial Revolution. Those wonderfully powerful machines and works of the late nineteenth and early twentieth centuries that transformed America into the leading industrial nation in the world are no longer in the vanguard. Today their importance is increasingly diminished as they are replaced by the often almost unfathomable scientific creations of the new "high tech" revolution that have brought us to the threshold of another cultural and economic age. It is perhaps not so much the new technology itself, as the rate of change; the pace at which it is transforming our lives that, more than anything else, differentiates this period of great innovation from others. However, there is no way of gauging at this point whether these changes will have as profound an effect on twenty-first century America as did the steam engine on the nineteenth and the automobile on the twentieth.

One cannot help but ponder the questions of whether the impact of high technology or even the automobile on our lives and sensibilities will ever be as great as that of the steam engine charging, hissing, and bellowing unannounced into the well-ordered pastoral landscapes of Constable or Cropsey. With a single stroke that event changed the course of history and civilization forever. It was like a Hadrian's Wall, which drew a line of demarcation between the ancient and modern world of technology. The steam engine quite literally pulled us out of the industrial dark ages and catapulted us into another, one that must have seemed even more improbable than landing on the moon did to the last generation. By it mankind was for the first time freed from his total dependence on wind and water and beasts of burden. Comparatively, the impact of computer technology on our lives and culture may not be as fundamental as that of the steam engine a century and a half ago. At least it is far too soon to tell. Once the industrialization was set in motion, everything that followed has been by comparison a matter of degree.

There are obviously very profound differences between the age of steam and this era. One of the greatest and most pronounced is the way in which things are made. Ours is an age of specialization, in which the realization of an idea often requires a far higher level of training and skill than in the past. The methods of production, too, have become more refined and automated than it was thought possible a generation ago. But much of what is produced today is made in ways that are largely unseen and too often unappreciated by most of us. Today technology and the industrial process do not often manifest themselves in forms as tangible as a steel mill or a great bridge.

It is, I believe, much more difficult now for most of us to be able to rejoice in our great achievements than it was for previous generations. Few of us know what it is to be there at a launching at Cape Canaveral. The rest of us can only "see" it secondhand on television, which so many have had to deputize as a surrogate for real experience. Today there are few events grand enough to stir our blood—events in which we can participate, such as the arrivals and departures one could witness a generation ago simply by strolling down to the depot at the foot of almost any main street in America.

Unquestionably technology has brought incalculable benefits. But these have not come without price. One of the most onerous has been an inflationary rate of dependence and willingness to abdicate our initiative to it. This point did not go unnoticed by many observers of the American scene even when the steam engine was barely able to totter its way along our primitive railway lines.

Emerson, who believed implicitly in our capabilities as a species, said only too prophetically, "Things are in the saddle, and ride mankind." And his neighbor Thoreau, who distrusted "things" even more profoundly, wrote:

> The nation itself...lives too fast. Men think that it is essential that the *Nation* have commerce, and export ice, and talk through a telephone, and ride thirty miles an hour..., but whether we should live like baboons or like men, is a little uncertain. If we do not get our sleepers, and forge rails, and

devote days and nights to the work, but go to tinkering upon our *lives*, to *improve them*, who will build railroads? And if the railroads are not built, how shall we get to Heaven in season? But if we stay at home and mind our business, who will want railroads? We do not ride on the railroad; it rides upon us.

More recently the noted Swiss historian Sigfried Giedion asked the question, "What does mechanization mean to man?" Answering it, he said,

> Mechanization is an agent, like water, fire, light. It is blind and without direction of its own. It must be canalized. Like the powers of nature, mechanization depends on man's capacity to make use of it and to protect himself against its inherent perils. Because mechanization sprang entirely from the mind of man, it is more dangerous to him. Being less easily controlled than natural forces, mechanization reacts on the senses and the mind of its creator.
>
> To control mechanization demands an unprecedented superiority over the instruments of production. It requires that everything be subordinated to human needs.

●   ●   ●

I FIND IT IRONIC that in spite of the unprecedented scientific accomplishments of this age, and the fact that man has garnered more knowledge so far in this century than in all the previous millennia of his existence, the places where these events take place so often give no outward clue to the significance of what takes place inside, much less mirrors its importance. The technology and ideas of the future, it appears, will never again require structures like blast furnaces. From a physical and visual point of view the work place no longer reflects the importance and nature of the work itself. The new industrial architecture and landscape are generally uninspired (save perhaps of NASA). The largest building in the world, where the 747 jumbo jet is manufactured, is just that—the largest building. It could be a warehouse. It is a gigantic shed that from the outside gives no indication of the importance of the work that takes place behind its walls. Its uniqueness rests solely with its immensity—the only thing that distinguishes it from thousands upon thousands of other similar structures.

In spite of the changing character of the industrial landscape, our image of industry does not yet seem to have caught up with the physical reality. It is not yet part of the iconography of our culture. Our perception of industry is still one of intensely dramatic places choked with smokestacks and steel mills and railroad yards, a world seething with obvious productivity, and sweat and grime. It is the place that Sandburg conjured for us—Chicago in the 1920s. We still perceive it in terms defined by John Chase's paintings, or the allegorical murals of Benton and those Diego Rivera painted in the thirties. The essence of Pittsburgh is still like the primitive canvases of a one-time steel worker, John Kane, or the photographs of Eugene Smith. But you can breathe a little more easily in Pittsburgh today—the air is relatively clean, because most of the mills are "down."

Reginald Marsh's etchings of tugboats and of the Erie Railroad yards in Jersey City and his murals of the harbor forever defined those places. Yet Marsh's New York harbor, once the most exciting place in the world, is today empty and lifeless. The steam tugs and ocean liners are gone.

I so often look with envy on the industrial photographs of Margaret Bourke-White, Andreas Feininger, those of Walker Evans, and those taken by Berenice Abbott in New York harbor. These people had a wealth of subject matter to deal with. Their work represents an extraordinary picture of American industry at its very apex revealed with all its contradictory implications. By contrast, the photographs I took for this book represent both the end point of one era and the beginning of another. In that sense, they are documents of change, indicative of the evolution that is taking place in our industrial landscape.

I have always felt that I have been standing on the middle ground between two eras, with one eye on the nineteenth century and the other on the twenty-first. This has been the vantage point, the place from which I have observed and photographed my country. My photographs can record the past. but for the future they can only project, and indicate a new direction. They cannot define it.

America moves at such a pace that we compress history. We have rushed at our land like a lion gorging on its prey. Since the beginning, we have raced toward the horizon; building, rebuilding, discarding. All across America we have left abandoned, like carcasses after the feast, that which only yesterday was state-of-the-art invention. Our land is littered with what in another culture might be viewed as the ruins of a civilization that had flourished a thousand years before, not a generation or two ago.

Technology, once we have committed ourselves to it, becomes a stern master, always experimenting; dictating, like Mengele, what shall survive and what shall go—and, it would seem, ultimately determining how we shall live and the course of civilization itself.

The difference in attitude between Europeans and Americans is so graphically revealed by the way each has treated its structures; by comparing the visual appearance of their land and ours. The continuity of civilization has been allowed to flourish in Europe. Europeans, in spite of routinely ravaging their countryside with periodic warfare, do not have a tradition of despoiling it with the detritus of a commercial civilization, trashing it as we do ours. Parisians and Londoners do not throw away their buildings as readily as Chicagoans and New Yorkers. In a land of such length and breadth as ours, Americans have never felt compelled to cherish our resources as much as the rest of the world has had to. Here there was always more; another place to go, or so it seemed. There was no compelling need to stay on, to fix up the old tractor or washing machine. The luxury of seemingly infinite choice, or another chance always beckoned.

Where will our culture have evolved in fifty years? Will our silicone valleys and industrial parks by then be ruins, as many of our industrial buildings are today? Judging by the shoddy construction of most contemporary buildings, I would venture to say that it might only be a matter of a few years before they fall into a state of woeful decay. Perhaps by the time we have finally come to accept these places as being part of our iconography they will be defunct, as Buffalo Bill in Cummins's *Portraits*. But I find it hard to believe that they will ever be perceived in the same way. There is little in those endless rows of sanitized, modular structures that would serve as an inspiration to any generation. Perhaps the enduring symbolism of the industrial world will always be those earlier, immensely compelling, smoky places.

•　　　•　　　•

It was purely by chance that I came to live near Chicago in the first place and later was given the opportunity to make these photographs. But I would have chosen Chicago anyway. There is no better place in this country to see the changing industrial landscape. Chicago is the right place, not only because of the size of its operations but because, unlike many of our other manufacturing centers, it is not a one-industry town. It is not as vulnerable to economic change as such places as Pittsburgh, Detroit, Waterbury, or Birmingham, whose fortunes were linked to a particular product such as steel or automobiles. However, Chicago, like other industrial cities in the northern tier of states, is suffering from a common malady. For years its economic base was founded on the heavy industries—steelmaking, the manufacturing of machines, automobiles, and the railroads—none of which is s important as it once was in the scheme of things. Chicago's industries, like those in the rest of America, are facing increased competition from the rest of the world, and increased labor and energy costs at home. As a result, many companies have consolidated their operations or pulled up stakes to relocate in the sunbelt, where so far labor is cheaper and the climate kinder than near the Great Lakes.

One need only drive from Gary, Indiana, the eastern gateway to Chicago, to O'Hare International Airport, northwest of the city, to see how dramatically the industrial landscape of America is changing. There in the space of an expressway hour one can see the transition from the world of coal, steel, and iron to the world of services and the microchip. But perhaps more than anything else it is the scale on which everything in Chicago seems to have been drawn that makes it the best place to look at American industry. It is built on the same scale as America.

Chicago is unique in another respect, too. It is built on an absolutely level plain, which spreads away from the lake surely to the edge of the western horizon. Because of its flatness everything that Chicago has built stands in bold relief against the sky. There are no hills behind which to hide its works, or valleys along which to take shelter. Everything is laid bare. The relationship of man and mechanization is dramatically played out. No other city that I know of reveals the industrial world on such a stage. Against all the rest, the Loop, downtown Chicago, one of the most powerful concentrations of architecture to be found anywhere in the world, has by comparison only a small role to play. When viewed from these industrial environs it has almost nothing to do with the rest of the city and stands aloof and shimmering, separate from the other city in the foreground. America is a country of great disparities, and nowhere can this be more graphically seen than in this juxtaposition. It seems quite natural too that it was in the Loop, the mother of the skyscraper, long before its effects were felt at the mill gates, that indications of the new industrial order to come first appeared in the form of corporate office buildings.

Once one turns his back on the skyscrapers, he can become lost. Once the hallmarks—the Sears Tower or the John Hancock Center—are out of sight, the working-class neighborhoods of Chicago become a generic place that belongs as well to our other old northern industrial cities. Although it is mostly an anonymous place—another generation's Centex Industrial Park—here and there we are brought back specifically to Chicago by a landmark, a Central Manufacturing district, or by Western Electric or A. Finkel and Sons. But for the most part it is the same interchangeable landscape that one sees from the train window approaching Cleveland or Newark or Buffalo or in the interminable environs of Philadelphia.

The photographs in this book are not intended to be a definitive study of American industry or even Chicago's. My intention was to give an impression of what the industrial environment is like, to show how it is changing, and to indicate what might evolve. The complexity and the number of locations available to choose from made it impossible to deal with every aspect of the subject. I did not set out to document each industry or process separately but to photograph only those that are most representative. The specific place was never considered as important to me as its generic or symbolic value. The photographs themselves have been arranged to reflect, at least conceptually, if not precisely, that drive from Gary to O'Hare; to mirror the transition from one world to another.

This book is the result of my lifelong preoccupation with man's works and his machines. To me it is a reflection of his complicated and often contradictory aspirations. My purpose has not been to eulogize, glorify, or damn. I am an observer here, and my approach has been that of an archeologist. If there is a point of view it is one of deep ambivalence about the industrial process and its effects on the course of civilization.

•   •   •

IT WOULD BE impossible to acknowledge all of the many people and concerns that helped me during the three years that I was involved in making these photographs. However, I would like to thank the Chicago Historical Society, without whose sponsorship and financial backing this project would never have come to fruition. I also owe a great debt of gratitude to Glenn Hansen, who, once again, as in many other cases, assisted me so unstintingly and ably with this project. And to Sandra, my wife, whose devotion and concern gave me encouragement and raised my spirits when they flagged. She knew, too, when to tell me it was time to stop and always provided a haven for me when I did. Thank you.

South of Chicago

Steel mills

Calumet River

Indiana Harbor Canal

4

Ore boat

Coke plant

Coke plant

Steel mill

Coke plant

Steel mill, ore bridges

Iron ore

Blast furnace

Steel mill sintering plant

Limestone crusher

Abandoned steel mill

Steel mill, high line

Steel mill, basic oxygen furnace

Steel rolling mill

Steel mill

Steel mill

Rolled steel

Steel mill, blast furnace casthouse

Steel mill, blast furnace casthouse

Steel mill, blast furnace casthouse

Steel mill, blast furnace casthouse

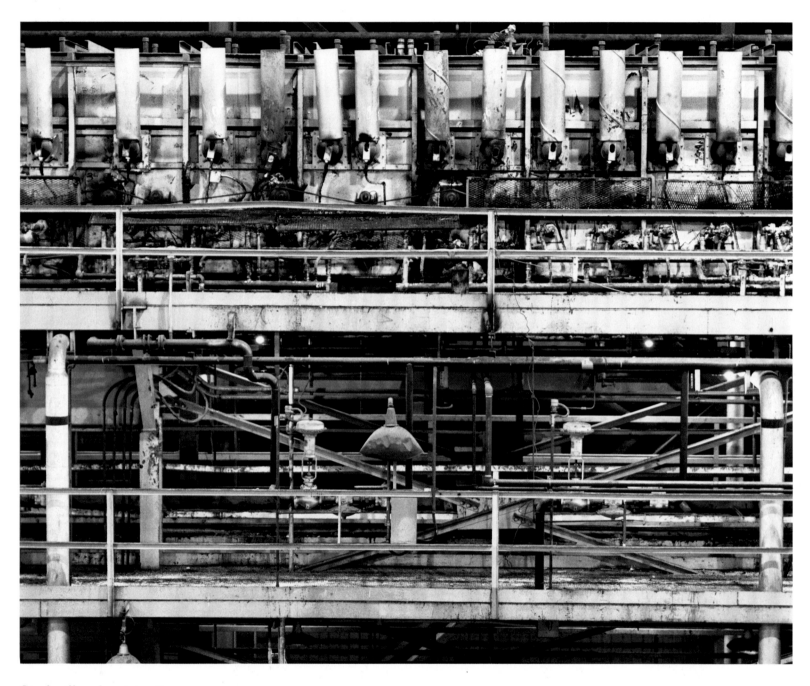

Steel mill, galvanizing line

Steel mill, galvanizing line

Automobile assembly line

Automobile assembly line

Automobile assembly line

Automobile assembly line

Automobile assembly line

Automobile assembly line

Steel mill

Washroom

Vending machines

Locker room

East Chicago, Indiana

Mill Gate, South Chicago

South Chicago

South Chicago

Oil refinery

Whiting, Indiana

Tank farm

44

Tank farm

Tank farm

Oil refinery

Oil refinery

48

Oil refinery

Grain elevator

50

Calumet River

Flour mill ventilators

Flour mill

Flour mill

Cereal plant

Grain elevator, ventilating fans

Grain elevator

Grain elevator

Grain elevator and barge

Freighter unloading steel

Port of Chicago, Lake Calumet

Abandoned malt house

Generating station

Generating station turbines

Generating station control room

Generating station

Sanitary and Ship Canal

Railroad yard

North of the Loop

Railroad yard

South of the Loop

Marktown, East Chicago, Indiana

South Chicago

South Chicago

South Chicago

South Chicago

Steel worker

South Chicago

78

South Chicago

Whiting, Indiana

Butcher

Stockyards

Stockyards

Slaughterhouse

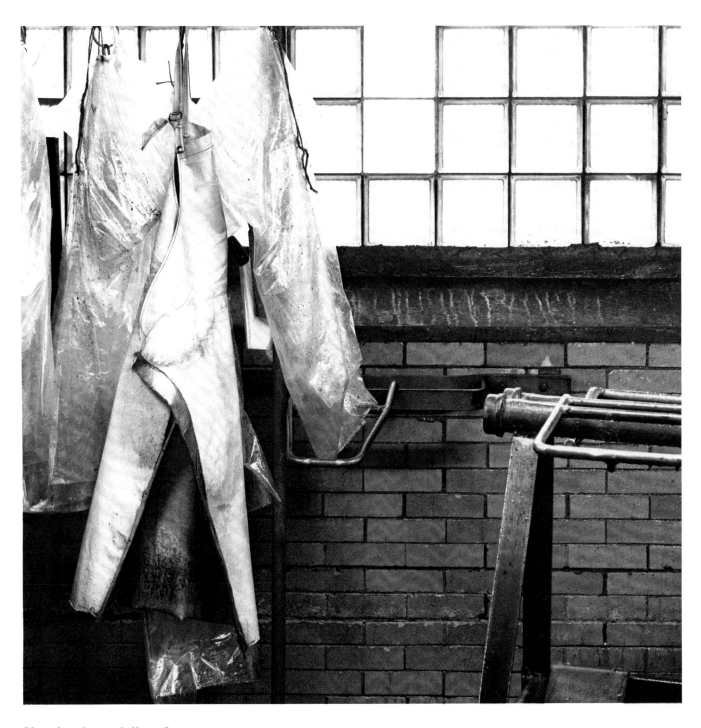

Slaughterhouse killing floor

Slaughterhouse killing floor

Slaughterhouse

Slaughterhouse killing floor

Stockyard

Central Manufacturing District

South of the Loop

North of the Loop

Central Manufacturing District

Underpass west of the Loop

Factory building north of the Loop

Scrap pile

Overpass west of the Loop

Bridge on North Branch of the Chicago River

West of the Loop

North of the Loop

Overpass west of the Loop

West of the Loop

Abandoned loading dock

East of the Loop

Sugar refinery

Industrial park

106

Industrial park

Diesel locomotive

Locomotive shop

Electric furnace shop

Foundry

Automobile assembly line

Electric furnace shop

Foundry

Wire mill

Lathe control

Control panel

Drill press

Press punch operator

Press room

120

Pressman

Printing plant sheet storage

Printing plant

Foundry worker

Blacksmith

Chemical storage area

Back of turbine

Truck yard

Industrial park

Industrial park

Loading ramp

Industrial park

Industrial park

Lunchroom wall

Lunchroom

Office, industrial park

Office worker

Assembly line checker

Assembly line

Office, industrial park

Nuclear generating station

Electronic controls

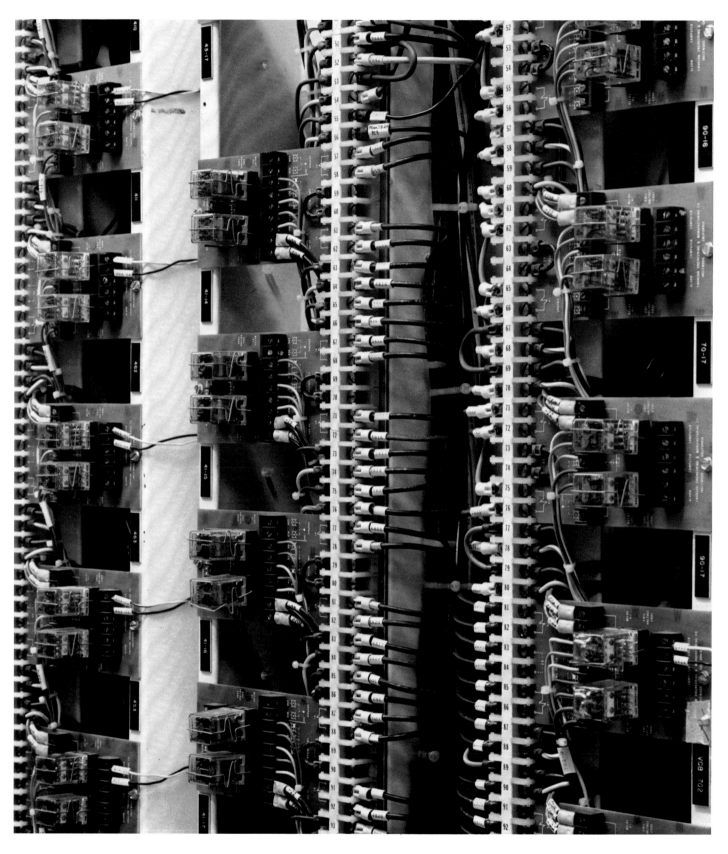

Relay panel

Nuclear generating station

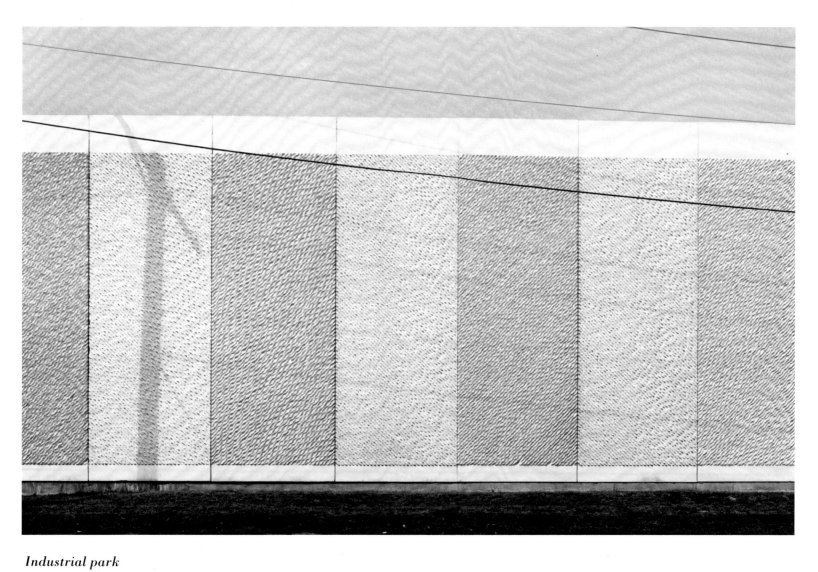

Industrial park

Industrial park

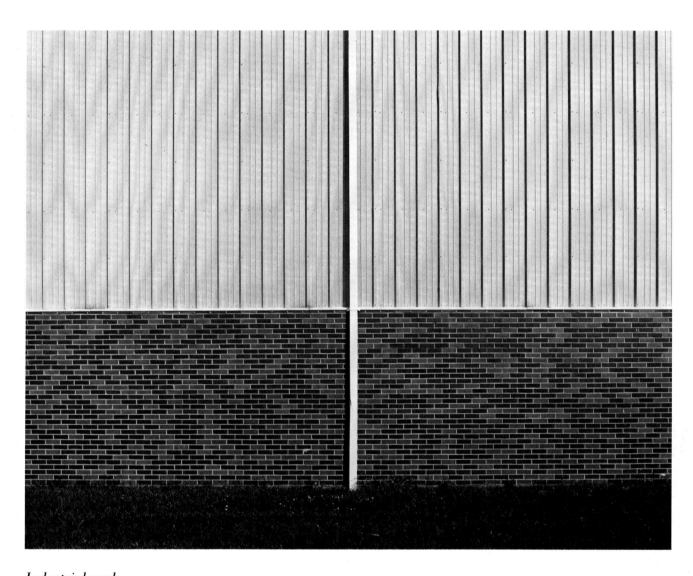

Industrial park

Abandoned grain elevator west of the Loop